Hazel Brown

A Very Special Vet

By Jupy James

Hazel Brown: A Very Special Vet
By Jupy James.
Copyright © Proverse Hong Kong, 16 October 2013, 20 November 2014, March 2021.
Second edition published in Hong Kong by Proverse Hong Kong, March 2021.
ISBN-13: 978-988-8492-27-5
First published in Hong Kong by Proverse Hong Kong, 20 November 2014.
ISBN 978-988-8227-00-6

First edition distribution (Hong Kong and worldwide):
The Chinese University Press, The Chinese University of Hong Kong,
Shatin, New Territories, Hong Kong SAR.
E-mail: cup@cuhk.edu.hk Web site: www.cup.cuhk.edu.hk
Distribution (United Kingdom): Stephen Inman, Worcester, UK.
Email: <ukagent@proversepublishing.com>
Enquiries: Proverse Hong Kong, P. O. Box 259, Tung Chung Post Office, Tung Chung, Lantau Island, NT,
Hong Kong SAR, China.
E-mail: proverse@netvigator.com Web site: www.proversepublishing.com

The right of Jupy James to be identified as the author of this work including text and illustrations
has been asserted by her in accordance with the Copyright, Designs and Patents Act 1988.

Page and cover design and layout by Jupy James.

British Library Cataloguing in Publication Data.
A catalogue record for this book is available from the British Library.

Proverse Hong Kong

Hazel Brown
A Very Special Vet

by

Jupy James

Proverse Hong kong

In a street near you there is a little shop called
Poorly Pets.

It is a very special kind of place.

If your pet is feeling sick and not very well,
this is the place to go.

Poorly Pets
OPEN
VET

Inside Poorly Pets works a man called Mr Brown.

Mr Brown is a very special kind of man because Mr Brown is a VET.

Vets help sick animals to feel better.

Mr Brown has a daughter who loves animals very much.

Her name is Hazel.

Every day after school Hazel helps her dad.

Together they can fix a broken wing,

heal a tender tummy,

and solve even the most unusual problems!

She helps her dad in lots of ways and she knows that being

a vet is a very special thing.

She dreams that one day she can be the thing that she wants

to be more than anything else.

She dreams that one day she can be a real vet.

Behind her dad's clinic is the garden.

It's where all the animals can play and relax until they

feel better.

Hazel loves the garden and she knows the names of all

the pets who play there.

When she walks out into the garden they always rush to

greet her.

One afternoon, Hazel threw a ball for Scruffy the dog.

It sailed over his head

and landed deep in the bushes.

Next to where the ball had landed, Hazel found the mouth

of a long dark tunnel.

Slowly they began to edge their way inside.

Hazel was a brave girl and not easily scared.

"I wonder where this will take us?" she thought.

They stepped out into an amazing animal paradise. It was a secret garden where all kinds of animals played, ran and swam.

Hazel had never seen so many animals and her heart was full

of joy to see them all so happy.

"What a fabulous place," thought Hazel,

but then she heard a growling and a

grumbling.

"Who can be unhappy in a place like this?" she wondered.

Just then an enormous leopard jumped out of the bushes!

It gave her an icy stare that made Hazel feel rather nervous,

until she noticed something quite odd.

"Leopards should not be grey," Hazel told the Leopard.

The leopard looked so sad that Hazel decided she had to help.

Then she had the most wonderful idea.

Back through the tunnel they crawled.

Back in her bedroom,

Hazel set to work with her

paints and brushes.

"Sit still," she told the leopard, "This might tickle."

It took Hazel a long time but at

last she finished.

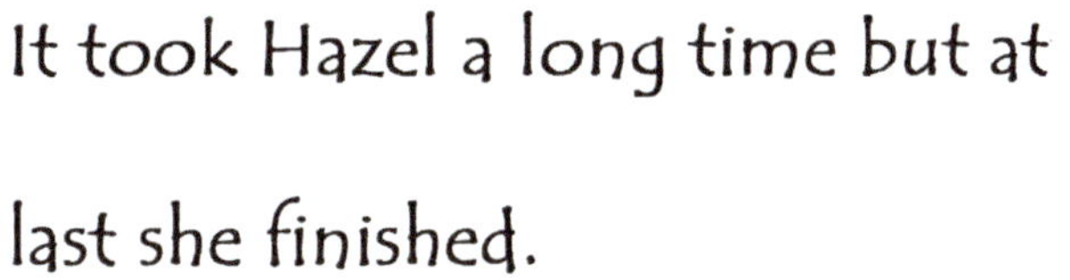

When the leopard saw his fabulous new

colours he could hardly recognise himself.

Proudly they rode back to the secret garden paradise.

The leopard no longer hid and growled.

He purred with pride as the other animals stopped and stared at

him and Hazel.

After that Hazel was very busy indeed.

"You really should watch your diet, Mr Snake!"

"What naughty mosquitoes,

Mrs Crocodile!"

"This will help your knee, Mr Peacock!"

Hazel had never been so happy.

The animals came from far

and wide to receive

her special care.

"Still no change Mr Chameleon?"

"No more fleas for you, Little Monkey!"

For Hazel it was a dream come true.

That night, when Mr and Mrs Brown went to say goodnight to Hazel, they found some strange footprints on the stairs.

HAZEL

When they opened the door, they were amazed to discover

that Hazel had become a very special vet indeed.